The Car Salesman's Bible

Ron Vest

ISBN-13: 978-1537235523
ISBN-10: 1537235524

DEDICATION

This book is dedicated to my best friend, my wife. Without her understanding, patience, support, and help this book would have never been possible.

CONTENTS

INTRODUCTION

My first job in the automobile industry was working for a group that had 10 dealerships, 5 on each side of the highway, and my job was not in sales. The gentleman that became my mentor, the vice-president of the group, came to me and said, "Ron, why don't you sell cars for me?" I said, "I don't want to be a car salesman." When he asked me why I said, "Because car salesman are liars, cheats and thieves and I don't want to be one." My mentor said, "What if I told you I would never ask you to lie, cheat or steal?" I made the decision, at that moment, that would guide my career for the rest of my life, I said, "Okay." Over the next 13 years he groomed me in all aspects of the car business and he never asked me to lie, cheat or steal.

The car business can be very tough. Especially in the beginning before you build your business. If you take the time to lay a great foundation it will get much easier and more profitable (and yes, you can make six figures as a professional car salesperson). I always thought that if I was going to be away from my family for 12 hours per day I would a) be the very best at what I did and b) someone was going to pay for all my hard work because I wasn't working for free. If I was going to be a professional I deserve to be paid like a professional.

One of the greatest compliments I have ever received came very unexpectedly. I had been in the car business for about 20 years and had personally trained over 300 salespeople. The same training you are about to receive. I was just hired as the general manager of a dealership and was holding my first meeting with the salespeople. I was making the point that following a process is extremely important and I listed the steps in the sales training that are in this book. One of the salespeople raised their hand, took out a folded up piece of paper, and read the steps of the sales process I had just listed. I asked him where he got that from and he said that salespeople had been passing it around for years because they never received better training from their employers. That is the reason for this book. To give the person who wants to be a professional car salesperson a map on how to achieve success. This book is very extensive and was written for the new hire as well as the seasoned pro.

I truly hope this becomes a tool that you use often and you have the discipline to follow the process. In other words, I hope this becomes The Car Salesman's Bible.

Best regards,
Ron

The Car Salesman's Bible

1. OVERVIEW

"The more you know about the past, the more prepared you are for the future" - Theodore Roosevelt

The History of the Car Business

The history of the automobile began in the 1880s when in 1886 in Germany Karl Benz registered the first patent in the industry for the first gas-powered vehicle. This "horseless carriage" was called The Motorwagen and from 1888 to 1893 around 25 Benz vehicles were sold. Meanwhile, the first commercial car sale was made by Charl and Frank Duryea in 1893. It was more a gas powered carriage than an automobile as we would understand it today.

By the end of the 19th century, Benz was the largest car company in the world manufacturing 572 vehicles in 1899. In 1903 France became the world's leading automaker, producing 30,124 cars (almost 49% of the global market). At the same time, the USA managed to manufacture only 11,235 cars.

For the duration of World War II, almost all car

manufacturers were forced to curtail production, reducing car sales dramatically. After the war ended, as soldiers returned to their hometowns, they started to buy cars. As rationing of metals and other components lessened, automotive production started to ramp up. This period of increased demand and supply is often referred to as the "car boom".

During the "car boom" there was no control over pricing for cars in dealerships. In 1958 Senator Almer Stillwell Monroney introduced legislation requiring dealerships to place a sticker on every car from any given manufacturer with a recommended retail price and a list of specifications. It came to be commonly known as the Monroney Sticker and was the most significant development in how cars were being sold. Fundamentally, it was the first regulation designed to protect consumers in the automotive industry.

Throughout the 50s and 60s the automotive market flourished. However, in the early 70s, due to the increasing price of gasoline, production costs rocketed, and customers were made to feel the pinch. To offset rising costs, car manufacturers slashed the number of models on the production line. Despite this, the cost of manufacturing kept increasing, forcing up car prices. As a result, dealers started to push the concept of leasing.

Prior to the 70s, consumers typically changed cars every 5-6 years. With the advent of car leasing, the average buying cycle decreased to 2-3 years. This sparked a revival in production that saw many different models entering the marketplace again. Together these factors led to the birth of the used-car market.

The next big change came in the 90s when the first wave of computer technologies became mainstays. Buyers started to shift to going online at the beginning of their shopping experience. Websites of dealerships, that at the beginning acted only as an online brochure, started to act as almost the whole online dealership. Everything was developing well until the financial crisis of 2007-2008.

2008 and 2009 were very hard years for the car industry. Total production dropped by 3.7% in 2008 and still further (by 12.4%) in 2009.

However, now, car sales and the automotive market in general has started to recover. In 2014, car sales started to bounce back and 16.52 million cars were sold. U.S. car sales in 2015 jumped 5.7%. In all, automakers sold 17.5 million cars and light trucks in the U.S. in 2015.

What is the future for dealers and consumers? How will the car buying experience change? The shift towards online sales and Omni-channel technologies is inevitable. But the human element remains a prevalent part of the sales process. Tangible experiences like sitting in a car, test driving, and talking with a salesperson are integral parts of the buyer journey.

The difference between "selling" the prospect and helping them to buy

People do not want to be "sold." They want to make their own choices and decisions and when they feel as though they are being manipulated or "pushed," they push back. Not good for building relationships huh? When I had been in the car business for a few years and wanted a fairly expensive widget I would "sell" my wife on the idea (or so I thought). Until one day she got tired of the whole mess and said: "Stop trying to sell me!" That's when I knew I had to change my process.

If my own mother needed a vehicle I would not "sell" her. I would determine her needs and help her to buy!

If you focus on helping the prospect to buy, the sale will come.

Stories sell, NOT price

There are more used vehicles sold in the U.S. through private parties than through dealerships. The reason? The interested party can get the story of the vehicle from the owner. They can find out what the vehicle was used for, how far they drove each day, who was the person driving? Can the person selling the vehicle lie? Sure they can but perception is a reality for the buyer and their perception is that dealerships can be dishonest. In a 2012 Gallup poll consumers rated car salespeople as the least trustworthy occupation. Next on the list was congressman! I do believe this is changing, as it should, and we should do everything in our power to dissuade this perception. Later, in the chapter on selection, I will illustrate the power of the story.

Professionalism

If you intend to make a professional income you should behave, and look, like a professional. Despite what the customer does or how the customer behaves, there are certain things you should never do and some you should always do.

Just some of those things are:
1. Do NOT curse or use foul language
2. Do NOT tell dirty or off-color jokes
3. Do NOT smoke
4. Do NOT become too friendly/comfortable with the customer
5. Do NOT be impolite
6. Always treat EVERY customer with respect
7. Always maintain decorum
8. Do NOT do anything you would not want your children to know you've done

In regard to how to dress; if your dealership has a dress code, follow it. If not, I suggest dressing one notch above how your average prospect dresses, without making them feel uncomfortable. We had a new salesperson who did not have a lot of money and our dress code dictated he wears a suit and tie each day. The salesperson only had one suit, one tie, and two dress shirts. He would wash his dress shirts every other night and no prospect was the wiser. He went on to become an extremely successful salesperson selling more than 30 vehicles per month. Needless to say, his business wardrobe dramatically increased.

Questions - the importance of who is asking

Two items to keep in mind regarding this subject: the first is, never ask a question you don't know the answer to; the second is, whoever asks the questions controls the conversation.

If I am on the showroom floor and listen to a salesperson take an inbound sales call and it sounds like this:

> Thank you for calling ABC dealership. How may I help you?
> Yes, we do carry those.
> We have 2 blue but no white.
> Okay, thank you.

Who do you think is in control of that call? The prospect of course.

Now, let's listen to a different spin:

> Thank you for calling ABC dealership. How may I help you?
> Yes, we have a great availability of those vehicles. Speaking of availability when would you be available to come into the dealership? Would today or tomorrow be better?
> Morning or afternoon?
> 2 or 3 o'clock?
> Do you have a pen and paper handy? Please write this down...V....E....S....T, that's my last name. My first name is Ron. Please ask for me when you come in and I'll let the receptionist know you're coming. If anything should come up and you can't make it in, please give me the courtesy of a call and I'll do the same.
> Great, I'll see you at 3 tomorrow.

Hear the difference? Remember, what we know in advance

we do in advance. 90% of the prospects are going to ask the same questions and say the same responses. Think through the conversation in advance and you'll be one step ahead.

The prospects' thoughts

Keep in mind that to the prospect this is a big decision. They don't buy a vehicle every day. They are full of apprehension, fear, and probably dread. They have been driving their trade-in for some time, they want to get rid of it for a reason, and when they walk onto the dealership property with 300 vehicles, they are like a kid in a candy store! The purpose of us controlling the prospect is the same reason a doctor controls the patient. It would not be the most effective way to achieve the prospect's desired result. Always keep in mind where the prospect's mind is. That apprehension, fear, and dread can and will, cause tempers to flare and rash decisions to be made. Understanding why they are acting the way they do helps us to deal with them in a customer focused way.

The importance of a process

Process: a series of actions or steps taken in order to achieve a particular end.

Through years of trial and error, all of the information in this book has been tried, tested and proven. This book is a series of steps that result in a sale, a process. McDonalds is built upon the process. When Ray Kroc, founder of the McDonalds franchise, sold a franchise it was under the agreement that every process would be adhered to. If a franchisee decided on their own to cook the burger for another 30 seconds beyond that set process, Mr. Kroc would pull their franchise. He had determined all of the processes necessary to drive the desired end result (success) and that is why every McDonalds you walk into today is exactly the same. Is this book the only way to successfully sell cars? No. But especially starting out, it's a terrific roadmap. If, in a year or two, you decide to change the process make sure you measure the result to ensure your success. Remember, if it matters, measure it. Nothing is good or bad until you compare it to something else.

Now that we have the right mindset, let's get down to business!!

2. PROSPECTING

"We are what we repeatedly do, excellence then is not an act, but a habit." — Aristotle

It would serve you well to have the thought process of an entrepreneur. Your own business inside a business. Drive your own leads and prospects and consider the advertising and marketing the dealership does as an added benefit. You have to continually fill your sales funnel to maintain consistent results. Don't be "a flash in the pan."

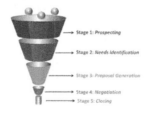

Here is what the average salesperson new to car sales goes through:

1) They prospect
2) Prospect sets appointment and arrives at the dealership
3) Salesperson uses the sales process to the letter

4) Salesperson continues the above for their first month and sells 12 vehicles

5) Salesperson thinks she/he has it all understood and starts to take shortcuts (including not prospecting nor following process)

6) Salesperson sells 2 cars the following month (the national average is 8)

7) Salesperson feels this business is not for them

8) Salesperson quits

Don't make this mistake!! You have to follow a proven process and this process starts with prospecting and continues indefinitely. This will ensure you feed the top of the funnel so that sales come out the bottom of the funnel. Neat how gravity works, huh? Prospecting is nothing more than convincing the prospect to give you the opportunity to help them buy a vehicle. People do things for their reasons, not ours. When you discover (through active listening) what their reason is and then appeal to that reasoning you will set the appointment. There are many, many books on prospecting. What I am attempting to do in this book is stress the importance of prospecting and share several ways to go about it. If you master prospecting, you will place yourself at a distinct advantage over other salespeople!

Below I have listed 7 ways to prospect. Start with these and I'm sure you will come up with others are your own.

1) "For Sale" sign in your personal vehicle

Place a "For Sale" sign in the back window of your (or your significant others) vehicle with your name and cell phone number on it. No, you are not lying. If someone offered you enough I'm sure you would sell it. But who will be calling you? Prospects! Explain to them you sell cars for a living and ask if that is the only type of vehicle they would consider? Remember, the one who asks the questions...

2) "Orphan owners"

Orphan owners are those customers that have purchased from the dealership previously and their salesperson is no longer working at the dealership. Ask management for a list of those owners so that you can "adopt" them. First, establish rapport with the customer. Send them a letter (along with your business card) letting them know their salesperson is no longer there and you would be happy to assist them if they have any questions or needs. Then after the letter has had time to arrive, follow-up with an introductory phone call and prospect the household. The phone script for prospecting the household is under the chapter on "Delivery."

3) Manufacturers list's

Manufacturers (Ford, Chrysler, Honda, etc.) frequently have lists of potential or current customers who the manufacturer has mailed an offer to (special interest rate, sale, incentives, etc.). Ask your manager for this list and follow-up with a phone call. The phone script for manufacturers list's is in the appendix at the end of the book.

4) Service department waiting room

According to CNBC, in July of 2015, the average person purchases or leases a new vehicle once every 6.5 years. Keep in mind that is an average. Knowing this wouldn't it be wise to prospect those people that are within a year to a year and a half of that time period? Well, your service department is full of them every day. Each night, check the appointment log in service to see which customers are bringing in vehicles that are 5 years old or older and will be waiting for it. Take down their name, time of appointment, and the year, make, and model of their vehicle. Check with your manager to see if they already have a salesperson and if they purchased it there, was it purchased new or used? You don't want to prospect a person about trading their vehicle they purchased a month ago. After they arrive, walk back and introduce yourself and start a conversation about their current vehicle and what type of vehicle they might be interested in if they were to trade.

5) Auto body shops

Everyone knows that body shops repair vehicles that are damaged. Some of those vehicles have sustained more damage than what the vehicle is worth (totaled). The person whose vehicle is totaled needs a new vehicle. That's where you come in. Visit local body shops, introduce yourself, leave some product information along with your business cards and let them know if they write their business name on the back of one of your business cards and send the prospect to see you (with the business card) about purchasing or leasing a new or used vehicle you would be more than happy to reciprocate and send them business also.

6) Insurance agents

Use the same technique that is used with body shops above.

7) Digital marketing

This is another subject that can fill numerous books and is continually changing. At one point in my career, I was a contract employee of Ford Motor Company working with their digital marketing department and it was a terrific learning experience. This entire area will be the subject of another book I am writing and will be more detailed and in-depth. Having said that, prospecting is a numbers game. The more quality material you associate with your brand, the greater your exposure. The greater your exposure, the more opportunity you have. The more opportunity you have, the more you sell and the more you sell, the more money you make. With one click you can send your message to 10,000 people. How powerful is that! You are your own brand. Expose it to as many people as you possibly can in the shortest time period possible and then continuously repeat. If you are not computer savvy, you should take some online lessons. Most are free and some are at a marginal cost. The Internet is not going away; it is your new showroom.

3. GREETING

"How you make people feel after they meet you is more important than what you say. Their experience with you becomes your business card." – Naveen Jain

How to prepare for an appointment

There are two ways in which you come face to face with a prospect. Appointments and walk-ins. Let's take a look at appointments first.

You have taken an incoming sales call and set the appointment for tomorrow. Great job! Since what we know in advance, we do in advance, we have some work to do. First, we know their name. Second, we know what time they are coming in (always be ready 2 hours in advance) and third, we know what they are interested in. Armed with this information take the following actions.

a) Make sure the vehicle you will be showing them is clean and ready to show. Back the vehicle they are interested in to the front door as close as possible (more about picking the right vehicle later). Print out an 8.5 by 11 piece of copy paper in landscape mode with something to the effect of "This vehicle reserved for Mr. and Mrs. Smith" typed, and place it inside the windshield on the driver's side.

b) Notify the receptionist and sales manager of your upcoming appointment. Then create a "welcome board" with the dealership's name, the prospect's name, the salesperson's name, and place inside the front door of the dealership. See the example below:

ABC Dealership
Welcomes
Mr. and Mrs. Smith
Your Salesperson,
Mary Jones
Is waiting for you!
Have a wonderful
visit!!!

If you want to get high-tech, buy a monitor and have the monitor become the "welcome board" with the above information. It makes a pretty impressive welcome when a large monitor is hung on the wall or from the ceiling welcoming the prospect.

c) Have the receptionist notify you when your appointment arrives and you notify the sales manager

d) Introduce your sales manager, who should welcome them to the dealership, and of course, introduce yourself.

e) Once the introductions are complete begin your sales process

• Imagine the impact the "reserved for" sign, the "welcome board" and the greeting from the sales manager has on your prospect. Talk about setting the stage!

Where, and how, to greet a walk-in prospect

A young man took the subway downtown every Sunday. He enjoyed this ritual because the subway was never busy on Sunday, was extremely quiet and he could read in peace. On one particular Sunday, a gentleman got onboard with his three sons. The sons were rambunctious and noisy, to say the least. They ran from seat to seat chasing each other and bumped into the young man twice as he was trying to read. After the third time they bumped into him, the young man could not hold his temper any longer. He stood and approached their father. "Sir, could you please control your children? They're running around yelling and have bumped into me three times and you haven't said a word." The gentleman broke out of a daze and apologized about his sons. In a whisper, the gentleman said to the young man, "We just came from the hospital. My wife, their mother, just passed away and I don't know how to tell them." Do you think that if the young man had known this he would have reacted differently to the boys, or maybe not reacted at all? Understanding why people do what they do does not necessarily make their actions okay. It does help us to deal with the situation in an informed manner.

Understanding why the prospect thinks the way they do is just as important. You need to know where they are coming from so you can deal with them appropriately and with empathy.

When the prospect enters your lot they are operating at some level, on fear. Fear that they will be "attacked", fear they will be taken advantage of or fear they will not negotiate well and pay too much. When you greet them, be at least six feet away and make eye contact. Smile. Treat them as a guest in your home and make them feel welcome. Remember, we are helping them to buy, not "selling" them and this is where it begins. Next, we will cover how to break down that fear-based barrier.

How to stop rapid fire questions

Inevitably you will run into the prospect that arrives on your lot or in your dealership, filled with fear. They want to get the process over with as quickly as possible. Their rapid fire rant will go something like this:

"I only have about twenty minutes. I want your best price on that blue pick-up, a value on my trade and don't try to steal it. Here are my keys and what interest rate are you gonna charge me?"

These type of individuals come across as intimidating but take a deep breath and relax. We understand why they are the way they are and we know how to handle the situation effectively. This should be your reply to gain control:

"I understand. Do you mind if I ask you a few quick questions so I can get you the information you want?"

Who would say no! You're offering to give them what they want if they give you what you want. Once they say yes, you now have control and you can begin your sales process as planned.

Breaking down the barrier

The last car dealership the prospect was at bombarded them with questions as soon as they walked on the lot. How much down? Are you trading? Where do you want your payments? Do you have good credit? The prospect feels as though they have been attacked! All of these questions need to be answered, but would you treat a guest at your home like this? Of course not. There is a natural progression that you will help guide the prospect through and get all these answers and more without the prospect feeling attacked.

A greeting is "Good Morning/Afternoon, how are you today?" It is not "Can I help you?" If you asked me that, I would say no because I am operating out of fear. Don't ask yes or no questions! After you ask them "How are you today?" you may get a response similar to, "We're just looking." This is also a fear based response to get rid of you. Remember we talked about questions and he/she who asks the question controls the conversation. It applies here also. If the prospect says, "Is it okay if we just look?" your response could be, "Well sure it is! Are you looking for a car, truck or SUV?" You have just answered their question with a question and they feel they have to respond! Let's suppose the prospect says, "An suv." Your reply can be, "We have a great selection of suv's." In a conversational tone ask them if they have been here before and/or have they worked with another salesperson here?

Let's take a break here and talk about a term called "skating." Skating is when you take another salesperson's potential or current prospect and it is extremely shady and unprofessional. Your dealership will have its own policy regarding what constitutes a prospect, or not a prospect and what constitutes skating. Follow it! If I greeted a prospect and they said they were working with another salesperson I would immediately go get that salesperson or, if that salesperson was off for the day, I would help the prospect just as if they were my own. What did I expect in return from the other salesperson for helping their prospect if they were off? I expected that salesperson to help my prospect in the same manner if I were off for the day and my prospect came in. I never wanted the other salespersons money, I wanted my money! Now, back to the process.

Continue your conversation about anything except buying a car (and politics or religion). Discuss the weather, events in the area, an uplifting news story, but for 3-5 minutes do not talk about buying a car. Doing this diverts their attention away from their fears and helps them to see you as a person, breaking down the barrier and making it easier for you to help them.

Getting them to your desk and why – (Failure to do this may cost you the sale)

As we said earlier, the prospect arrives on your lot after driving their trade-in for 5 to 6 years and can't wait to get a new vehicle. They pull up amid 20 acres of cars, trucks and suv's and are overwhelmed. It's like a kid in a candy store! Left to their own devices, and allowed to control the process, they will cause you to lose the sale! Here's how:

The prospect is greeted by a salesperson who asks, "Would you like all the power options?" "Sure!" says the prospect. "How about a moon roof?" "Sure!" says the prospect. "And a ten-disc CD changer?" "Absolutely!" the prospect responds. They have been driving a crippled automobile and want every creature comfort available. Especially if they do not see any negative consequences for quenching that thirst. If the salesperson asked them, "Would you like all the power options which will add $120 per month to your monthly payment?" Do you think the prospect would be so enthusiastic to accept those options? I doubt it, but let's continue down this path and see what happens. The prospect and salesperson climb into the decked out vehicle and take a demonstration drive. They pull back into the dealership lot, get out of the decked out vehicle (that is parked right by their old trade-in), and the salesperson asks, "If my manager can fit this vehicle into your budget would you trade today?" The prospect says, "Heck yeah!" Duh! Why wouldn't they? They go inside, set down at the salesperson's desk, negotiate the deal and all the salesperson can get out of them is, "We need to think about it and we'll let you know tomorrow." Finally, the salesperson gives up, thanks the prospect for visiting and says that he/she will call them tomorrow to answer any questions. The prospect leaves.

The next day the sales manager overhears the salesperson's portion of a telephone conversation with the prospects from the day before and this is what the sales manager hears:

> Salesperson – "I just wanted to call and thank you for spending time with me yesterday and see if you have any questions?"
>
> Salesperson – "You did? Why? Was it something I did?"
>
> Salesperson – "Okay, well thank you again for your time and if I can help in the future please don't hesitate to call."

Yes, they had bought a vehicle somewhere else. Here is why. The prospects had decided what their budget for a monthly payment was the night before they visited that first dealership. They evidently chose a vehicle that was way out of their budget. When the salesperson presented the first monthly payment it was $280 per month higher than their budget. The prospects could hardly speak. The salesperson went back to his sales manager and when he/she came back the monthly payment was $265 more than their budget. They could not tell the salesperson that this was way beyond their budget and "save face" so they just said that they had to think about it and they left.

They went to the same type of dealership, in the next city over, knowing they could not afford all of the bells and whistles. They picked out a vehicle with a lot less equipment, the payment fell pretty close to their budget and they bought the vehicle. The first salesman lost the deal within the first 20 minutes of meeting the prospect. Here is how to avoid that from happening to you:

> a) After greeting the prospect say something similar to:
>
> "We have over XXX vehicles on our lot and they're not always organized well. Why don't we walk inside, have a seat and let me get a clear picture of what you want and need in your next vehicle? Once we accomplish that, I'll pull up a vehicle that fits your requirements and you

won't have to walk around the lot for hours.
Follow me! Start walking and don't turn around!

b)   After having your prospects take a seat at your
desk, offer them a refreshment (just like a guest
in your home).

c)   Take out a pen and pad of paper and get ready.

This leads us to our next chapter, qualification!

4. QUALIFICATION

When I use the term "qualification" in this book I am not referring to qualifying the prospect to determine whether they can buy or not. That is actually pre-qualifying. Don't do that to yourself! Let management and/or the banks qualify your prospect. Your job is to help the prospect buy. You may think that if you can figure out a way to pre-qualify a prospect without going through all of the steps of a sale, you will make more sales. Not so! One reason is, you never know what your management or the banks will do. Another reason is, even if they cannot buy they are a great source for referrals. If the prospect feels you have done everything in your power to help them buy, they will feel indebted to you and be more than happy to refer prospects to you. It's called the law of reciprocity and it works! Plus, if you keep in touch with them, when they can buy you will be the one they come to. It is money in the bank! You are qualifying what they are interested in, trading in and getting some personal information to better assist them.

People do not care how much you know until they know how much you care. The following questions are a guide for you. They should be asked in a conversational tone, not an interrogative tone. Attempt to truly understand their wants and needs but make sure you differentiate between these two. It is imperative that you fulfill their needs, it is nice if you can fill some of their wants. If you try to fill all of their wants AND needs, chances are you will experience our earlier catastrophe of trying to fit too much vehicle in their $400 per month budget and lose the deal.

Make sure you note the prospects' responses, it demonstrates caring!

Typical questions
a) Interested in
i.   What type of vehicle are you interested in?
ii. 2 door or 4 door/2WD or 4WD
iii. Automatic or 5 speed
iv. What will you be using the vehicle for?
v.   Do you prefer lighter or darker shades? If you ask them "What color do you want?" and they say "red" Murphy's Law says you will have everything but red in-stock!
vi. What type of equipment would you like?
vii. If there were a similar car, with similar equipment, would you consider it if we could save you some money? The purpose of asking this question is to see if the prospect is flexible and if we have more than one choice in finding them a vehicle that fits. If they ask "What do you mean?" you can say "I just want to know if you are open to a demonstrator or late model pre-owned."

b) Trading-in
i.   What year, make, and model is your trade-in? The reason you do not ask if they are trading is because they may have been told, possibly unjustly, that they will get a better deal if they

"hide" their trade-in until after they get a price on the new vehicle. Can you imagine what would happen if they didn't tell their doctor all their symptoms because they thought they would be charged more!

ii. When did you buy the trade-in? If the prospect says their trade is a 2014 do not assume they purchased it in 2014. The could have purchased it used 6 months ago which puts an entirely different set of factors into the equation!

iii. Did you finance or pay cash?

iv. If financed: What is the balance owed?

v. Who is the balance owed to? If the dealership does business with the lender they have financed through, let the prospect know that your dealership does business with them also. It sets the stage for the dealership to handle the financing of the new vehicle.

vi. If there were one thing you could change about your trade-in what would it be? Whatever they say when asked this question is what their next vehicle better have. If they say "I wish it had more room" than the vehicle you pick for them better have more room. Make sense?

c) Personal

The purpose of asking these questions is not to "profile" the prospect and pass judgment on them. The purpose of the questions is to determine how best to communicate with the prospect. It is similar to Maslow's Hierarchy of Needs. Maslow's Hierarchy of Needs relates to an individual's motivational level; the questions here relate to an individual's communication level, such as:

i. Where do you live? Not what city, but what neighborhood.

ii. What type of work do you do? Not where do you work, but what type of work you do.

iii. How much, in addition to taxes and tags, will you be putting down? The more money a person puts down the lower the monthly payment. The lower the monthly payment the greater the probability of approved financing and making the sale. Do not ask "Will you be putting anything down?" Remember, no yes or no questions, you'll get a "no" when you want a "yes."

iv. What range did you have in mind for a monthly investment?........Up to? Two items to mention here: we are asking for a range, $350 - $400, not a specific payment; next, after they give us a range we ask, "Up to?" and then we wait for the response. You will be amazed at how many times they will give an extra 10-15 dollars per month to work with.

v. Will there be anyone else helping to make the decision about your purchase? If they say yes and that person is not present say "Why don't we pick out something you think they'll like and we'll take a ride over and show them, okay?" This stops them from bringing this up in the close to get away from giving a commitment.

At this point we have a very clear picture of what the prospect is interested in, trading in, and some personal information to help the prospect buy. Now we move on to the selection.

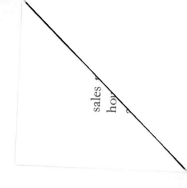
5. SELECTION

When you have completed the qualification it is time to pick a vehicle to demonstrate to them. You may want to take the information you have gathered to your sales manager for an opinion or use the information yourself to make a decision. Either way, make your prospect comfortable by offering more refreshments, letting them know where the restroom is, or offering your "Why Buy From Me" book. This is a book that you have created that gives the prospect reasons to buy from you. One of the strongest motivators to buy from you are previous customer testimonials. We will discuss how to effectively get customer testimonials in the chapter on follow-up. You can also include any certifications you have received, any awards you've gotten, any community recognition, etc.

Less is better than more

The lower the price of a commodity the greater the potential market share! If you gave your friend a gift for their birthday, how hard would it be for you to take it away from them? It's the same way with the model or equipment of a vehicle your prospect wants. Start with less and then go to more if you have to. So many times as a manager, I would speak with the prospect (after an hour of negotiations through the salesperson) in an attempt to get them to pay $20-$30 more in monthly payment only to find out they really didn't need the moonroof. We switched to a vehicle with no moonroof and closed the deal.

In order to understand the importance of "stories" in car sales, I want to tell you a quick story related to selling used vehicles.

Suppose you are shopping for a car and I'm your salesperson. I greet you on the pre-owned lot and notice you are looking at two identical cars side-by-side. The same year, make, model, mileage, equipment, and color. You ask me what I can tell you about these cars. I say:

"Well, car "A" we purchased at the auction. We performed a 150-point inspection on the vehicle and reconditioned it to very high standards. We also ran a Carfax on the vehicle and, as far as we know, the vehicle has not been reported in an accident. It's a very nice vehicle."

"Car "B" was purchased here as a new vehicle by a great young couple. They have had all of their maintenance work done here and we can show you the records. They have not had so much as a ding on their vehicle. They had to trade it in on a minivan because they had twins and needed more room. They loved the vehicle and said they would be happy to give it a great send-off to anyone who was interested in buying it."

Now, hearing the story, which car would you buy if the price were the same, car "A" or car "B"? Car "B" right? Of course! You would probably buy car "B" if it were $500-$1,000 more! Stories sell cars, not the price! Don't you think we would have a very high probability of a sale if we "picked" car "B"? I do. That's the importance of the "pick."

Placement of the "pick" and presentation

If you had an appointment, we would already have the vehicle of interest positioned with a "reserved for" sign in the windshield. If not, make sure the "pick" is presentable, the radio and windshield wipers are turned off, the driver and passenger front seat are placed all the way back (giving the most leg room) and the heat or a/c is on to make it comfortable.

Back the "pick" next to the prospect's trade-in, because nothing is good or bad unless it is compared to something.

Bring the prospect outside and introduce them to their next vehicle. Now, it's time to show the prospect why they should spend tens of thousands of dollars on a metal box. Next, the feature-benefit presentation.

6. FEATURE-BENEFIT PRESENTATION

The 5-step walk-around

The purpose of the walk-around is to build value. To help the prospect see why they should spend their hard-earned money on the vehicle you are presenting. This is one of the most skipped steps in the process because of time. If you skip this step, at best it will cost you gross profit, at worst it will cost you a deal. People do not buy your product; they buy what your product does for them. If they do not know what it can do for them, how much do you expect them to pay?

A few tips here. Make the presentation relevant to the prospect. If they are focused on safety, make sure you highlight safety items. If they are focused on performance, make sure you highlight performance. This is where the information we collected in qualification comes into play and is valuable. Another tip, don't sell what it doesn't have! If you sell anti-lock brakes, and the vehicle is not equipped with anti-lock brakes, you will have a problem.

Make sure you follow every feature with a benefit. If you tell me a vehicle has a dual master cylinder braking system (feature) it has no value to me if I don't know what that is. If you explain that it has two brake lines so that if one fails, you still have equal braking pressure (benefit) now it has value. Even though every vehicle has a dual master cylinder braking system, you are the only salesperson that has pointed it out. Therefore, the prospect will buy YOUR vehicle with that benefit instead of your competitors! The logical progression of this walk-around also allows you to cover all the external areas of the vehicle and leads naturally to a demonstration drive. Statistics show that a demonstration drive significantly increases the likelihood of a sale, so don't ask if they would like one, just do it!

I will give you the location of the 5 steps and some feature-benefits to point out in each area. Remember, don't sell what it doesn't have and KNOW your product knowledge!

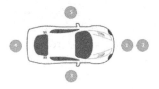

Position One: Front of car, hood open

Feature – Crimp points in the hood.

Benefit – Upon a front end collision the hood will collapse like an accordion versus entering the passenger compartment.

Feature – Dual master cylinder braking system.

Benefit – The braking system has two brake lines so that if one fails, you still have equal braking pressure.

Feature – Hood Insulation.

Benefit – Dampens noise and if the engine should catch fire, the "insulation" is released and smothers the fire.

Position Two: Hood closed, one step back from position one

Feature – Energy absorbing bumpers.

Benefit – Can withstand impacts twice that mandated by the federal government without causing major damage.

Feature – Wrap-around turn signals.

Benefit – Vehicles approaching from the left or right can easily see your intention to turn which helps avoid collisions.

Feature – Polyurethane bumpers.

Benefit – Reduces overall weight, which increases fuel economy and is less expensive to repair in the event of a collision.

Position Three: Passenger side of the vehicle

Feature – Door-in-roof design.

Benefit - Built in drip guard and increased aerodynamics to increase fuel economy.

Feature – Fold-away outside rearview mirrors.

Benefit – Mirrors fold backward/forward upon impact with an object to prevent the need for replacement or repair.

Feature – Recessed door handles.

Benefit – Hides scratches from continuous opening and closing of doors preserving the aesthetics of the vehicle and assisting in increasing resale value.

Position Four: Rear of vehicle, trunk open/closed

Feature – Fully carpeted trunk.

Benefit – Protects luggage and valuables that are in the trunk.

Feature – Space saving spare tire

Benefit – Lighter in weight and easier to change

Feature – Center mounted rear stop light

Benefit – Reduces rear-end collisions by up to 50%

Position Five: Drivers side of vehicle
Open the driver's door, offer the primary driver a seat so that you can explain the operating controls, open the passenger front door, offer the secondary driver a seat and you get in the back seat and explain the control panel from left to right.

Now for the demonstration drive.

7. DEMONSTRATION DRIVE

This is NOT a test drive. The vehicles were tested at the factory and they are fine.

Many salespeople feel it's okay to not accompany the prospect on the demonstration drive. They feel it's a waste of time to go on a ride. Let me tell you why I don't believe that. At one time there was a very popular automobile manufacturer who made improvements to their transmissions. Imagine two sets of gears interlocking. Every time the vehicle changes from first to second gear, second gear to third gear, and so on, this manufacturer made those gears "click" into place rather than sliding into place as other transmissions did. The result was gears that lasted much longer because they were not rubbing together and wearing down prematurely. The negative side of this achievement was that when the gears "clicked" into place it would cause a sudden jerk when shifting gears. If this were not explained to the prospect during the demonstration drive, they assumed something was wrong with this brand new vehicle, they would come back to the dealership, not mention it to the salesperson and leave. I have spent quite a bit of time explaining this because if an objection arises, and you are not there to overcome it, you may very well lose the opportunity. Remember, it is not reality that is important, but the prospects' perception of reality that matters. If you are not there to tighten the gap between perception and reality the prospects' perception will win out. Now back to our demonstration drive.

During the process of developing a relationship with your prospect, you will be able to determine who this vehicle is for, the primary driver (if it's a couple). Instruct the primary driver to slip the vehicle into drive and begin the demonstration drive. Discuss the prospects interest in the vehicle and overcome any objections that may arise. On the demonstration drive, at the half-way point, park and have the primary and secondary driver switch positions as you direct them back to the dealership and have them park in the "sold" area. The sold area is in the prospects' mind. You are taking their temperature to evaluate their propensity to buy now. If they question the "sold" area, explain that the "sold" area is an area where customers park so no one else can purchase the vehicle they are interested in.

• Note – There is an alternative (although not as smooth) method of ending the walk-around and beginning the demonstration drive. Have the primary driver get in the passenger seat, the secondary driver in the back seat while you drive out of the dealership. This allows you to maintain control of the route taken and lessons the risk of the prospect adjusting controls while driving resulting in a possible collision. At the half-way point, pull over and have the primary driver drive and the secondary driver in the passenger front seat as you direct them back to the dealership. Please follow your dealerships preference for who drives off the dealership property.

The silent walk-around of the trade-in

The purpose of the silent walk-around is to silently point out areas of deficiency on their trade-in and subconsciously devalue what they feel their trade-in is worth to more closely align their expectations with reality.

Begin by asking the prospect to "sell" you their trade-in. When was maintenance completed? Do they have maintenance records? Was it ever involved in an accident? Are they the only owner? When were the tires last replaced? If they mention anything negative ask them not to tell you, your manager will find that out. Then walk around the entire vehicle. Touch each scuff mark, dent, glass chip or balding tire. Look inside the vehicle. Prospects tend to have an overinflated perception of what their trade is worth. Each time you touch a flaw on their vehicle that perceived value takes a drop. Remember, don't say a word!

Trial close

Once the silent walk-around is complete ask the prospect, "If my manager can fit this vehicle in your budget would you trade today?" The purpose of asking this is three-fold. First, it surfaces objections that indicate you are showing them the wrong vehicle. The prospect may say "It doesn't have as much room as we thought it would" or "We were hoping it had more power." You want to find out if there is a problem with the "pick" now versus during the close. Second, if they say yes, you have identified that other than the budget, they are ready to buy. Lastly, they may tell you exactly how to close them. If they say, "Well, only if he gives us $XX,XXX for our trade" or "As long as my payment is not over $XXX per month." Surface, and overcome, as many objections as you can now so you don't slow down the process when you begin to close!

What if? What if you ask the trial close and the prospect says, "Absolutely not! We are going to three more dealers and two different makes and we will make a decision then." There are two schools of thought. My feeling is every step you take is another step toward selling a vehicle. The more engaged the prospect, the higher the probability of a sale. I would continue the sales process all the way through, including pricing, and try to surface why they feel they have to shop more dealers/models. Others feel that if the prospect does not commit at this point they should not be given pricing to shop with. But, if you were shopping for a product, and a store would not give you a price, would you return to buy from them? Regardless of your answer to that question, leave that decision to your management and follow their policy.

8. SERVICE AND PARTS DEPARTMENT TOUR

So far you have built value in yourself by not acting like a "car salesman" and truly caring about the prospect. You have built value in the vehicle they are interested in by performing a thorough feature-benefit presentation. Now it's time to build value in the dealership. To set your company apart from other dealerships. What makes your dealership unique - not only in the equipment you have, but also how the dealership cares about the customer through actions and not just talk. Once you have completed the demonstration drive, invite the prospect inside and offer them refreshments. Let them know that you would like to show them an area of the dealership that you are very proud of, your service and parts department.

The sales department sells the first vehicle, service and parts sell the rest

As a professional salesperson, service and parts can be your best friend. They will nurture your customer after you have sold them. You can help facilitate this nurturing, but the responsibility falls on service and parts. When the sales department sells a vehicle the customer is usually happy and excited. When they go to the service department it is because they have a problem with their vehicle or they are having regular maintenance performed. Either way, it is going to cost them. Either in money, time or both and they don't like it. Get to know your service and parts manager, the service writers, the receptionist and the technicians. I used to buy the techs pizza once a month to show my appreciation. Do you think I could get a customer squeezed in when I needed to? Plus, if the tech had a customer that needed a new or pre-owned vehicle, who do you think they sent them to? It may seem trivial now but do not underestimate the importance of your service and parts department, they really are invaluable.

Building even more value

People do things based on their reasons, not ours. Just like there are features and benefits on the vehicle, there are features and benefits in the service and parts departments. Do not mention a feature without mentioning the benefit.

Service and parts manager introductions

Introduce your prospects to both your service and parts manager. Let them know the combined years of service these managers have. Ask the managers for their business cards to give to your prospect. All of this is to make the prospect feel more at home before they have even purchased!

Hours of operation

Does this service department have evening or weekend hours of operation for the convenience of the customer? If so, let them know, because another dealership may not (and probably has not) told them about this.

Complimentary services

The following are complimentary services that are provided by some dealerships. As stated earlier, if your dealership doesn't have it, don't sell it!

Complimentary service – Drop-off service to work or home.

Benefit – The customer can drop their vehicle off at the dealership for their service appointment and a dealership employee will take them to their work or home.

Complimentary service – Night key drop-off.

Benefit – The customer can drop-off their vehicle the night before their appointment.

Complimentary service – Car wash.

Benefit – A nice clean vehicle when they pick their vehicle up.

Special equipment and training

In many small repair facilities (and some dealerships) their special equipment is extremely limited due to financial constraints. An alignment machine can cost in excess of $30,000 and that's not including special tools! This makes it necessary for these establishments to send that type of work out. This causes a delay for the customer. Most manufacturers, Ford, Chrysler, Honda, require that the franchised dealer also maintain an inventory of special tools that are specific to that manufacturer's models. Get a list of your special equipment that your dealership has from your service manager.

The manufacturers also require specialized training for the dealership technicians. Without their techs being "certified" by the manufacturer, the manufacturer will not pay for warranty work performed by non-certified techs! Usually, there are tech specific certifications hanging on the wall in the service department.

What it means to become part of the dealership family

In the dealerships that I ran as a general manager, we would have a "mom and pop" rule. If there was a customer with a problem, we would apply this rule. If it were your mom or pop sitting in front of you, and they had this problem, how would you resolve it? The answer to this question is probably the right thing to do. That's being part of the dealership family! Sewell Cadillac of Dallas, at one point, would have their prospects watch a 25-minute video of what it meant to be part of the Sewell Cadillac family. Sewell also had a fleet of 100 loaner vehicles for their service customers before it was standard practice in the industry. Your customer must get the feeling that they are part of something special because they are something special!

9. APPRAISAL & WRITE-UP

At the time of this writing, if you went to Kelley Blue Book online (KBB.com) and entered a 2010 Ford Taurus with average mileage, average condition, and standard equipment, Kelley Blue Book would value that vehicle within a $1500 range. That does not account for changes in condition or equipment that the prospect could make and would result in an even larger discrepancy. Is there any wonder why the trade-in value is the largest area of contention in a car deal between the prospect and dealership? Every dealership has its own appraisal process. Please follow that process if it deviates from this one.

Needed items

Most dealerships have an appraisal form that you should complete. In addition, the following is a list of items that should be obtained from the owner of the trade-in prior to taking the appraisal form to your manager:

a) The registration.
b) The title if they have it. Some states have a two-part title and some only one part.
c) Any maintenance records that the prospect has.
d) If the vehicle has been involved in an accident, a

copy of the body shop repair order listing the repairs completed.

e)   A copy of the original window sticker, if available.

f)   A complete payoff verification form, if there is a payoff on the trade-in.

g)   Make sure to write down the vehicle identification number (VIN) taken from the driver's side of the windshield, double check it and then compare it to the VIN on the driver side front door jamb or inside the glove box. The VIN has a tremendous amount of information related to the vehicle in addition to verifying it is the stated car. It's very important to make sure you have written this number correctly. DO NOT TAKE THE VIN OFF OF THE REGISTRATION.

h)   And of course, the keys.

Why you're working for them

If the prospect thinks that you are in control of the value that is placed on their vehicle, you are going to have a tough time getting them to trust and open up to you. You must let the prospect know you are working for them. If they do not buy, you do not get paid. Do not use phrases such as "I can give you $XX,XXX for your trade" or "If I could give you $XXX more for your vehicle would you buy now?" Remove the word "I" from these types of discussions. The proper way to say the above would be, "Great news! My manager can give you $XX,XXX for your trade," or, "If my manager gave you $XXX more for your vehicle would you buy now?" Words are very powerful. It is not necessarily what you say, but how you say it that matters. I can say, "You are so beautiful that when I saw you time stood still" or I could say, "I love ya to death but your face could stop a clock." In both instances I said the same thing, that time stopped. The only thing that changed was how I said it. Words are powerful!

Commitment or no commitment, both sides of the coin

Here is another area where there are two polar opposite thought processes. You are preparing to get the prospect's trade-in appraised and/or get figures to serve to the prospect for the purchase of the vehicle. Some feel as though you should get a commitment to buy now at a specific trade difference, selling price or payment (more on the different types of buyers in the chapter on closing) from the prospect to get them over the psychological hump of committing to purchase. Others feel that they do not want the prospect to commit because the prospect may lock the offer they give in memory and then you have an uphill battle from the beginning. Again, if your dealership has a process for getting, or not getting a commitment, please follow it. If the choice is yours, read the rest of this book before you make a decision on which way to go.

10. THE CLOSE

Emotion is a strong driver of human behavior. It can cause people to do illogical things at inopportune moments. An emotional prospect can be your friend or your enemy.

Closure principle: We seek closure as a release from tension.
How it works: Closure is the resolution of tension

One of the characterizing factors about tension is that when we experience it, we will drive towards its resolution. When we are threatened, we will seek the closure of safety. When we are watching an exciting crime film, we find satisfaction in the closure of knowing "who dunnit."

In buying, looking at something I want builds the tension of wanting. Completing the purchase creates the pleasure of closure.

Even death can be a welcome closure, as condemned people and the terminally ill well know.

Anticipation of closure creates pleasure

The pleasure of tension is in the anticipation of closure. A roller-coaster is a series of tensions as you crank up the slope, anticipating the drop the other side. As you reach the summit, there is a relief at having reached the edge, followed instantly by "will I survive" tension as you plummet over the edge, with the closure of relief as you reach the other end safely.

When shopping, we enjoy the pleasure of anticipated completion of the purchase.

The closer the closure, the greater the tension

When closure seems a long way off, then the tension is less. As closure approaches, tension increases exponentially. This can be seen in the excitement when a race is nearing conclusion or we are just about to find out who the murderer is in a detective story. This last-minute tension can be unbearable and cause us to take significant risks and raise the priority of reaching closure. It also explains why salespeople are constantly pushing towards closure, making it seem as if we are just about to own the product on sale.

Any closure can help any tension

When someone makes me tense by shouting or disobeying me, there are more ways of resolving this tension other than direct interaction with them. Slamming the door helps. So does driving fast and chopping wood. It's almost like we create other tension and subsequent closure in order to try and snag the broader closure.

Closure fills in the gaps

Because in closure we get to completion, if there are any gaps left, our minds will helpfully fill them in, like connecting a dotted line.

This is important for our everyday understanding

and processing of the world around us. We very seldom get complete information so we need to fill in the gaps on a moment-by-moment basis. Our models help us do this by helping us guess what is in the gaps.

Closure often uses assumption. For example, if we are buying a fridge and have the tension of not knowing if it will fit in the kitchen, we close this tension (and so decide to buy) by assuming that it will.

Closure closes the doors of the past

The closure is a literal event in more than one way. When we experience closure, we close the doors on the confusion of the past. Closed doors let you focus on the future. They let you decide quickly in the future. Closed doors are also hard to open again.

Two types of closure: aha and yes

Closure happens in two places during a person's thinking.

First, when you understand, and meaning is created, you close the doors on any further pondering of what your experience means. Legend has it that Archimedes when asked to determine the value of the Syracuse king's crown, went for a bath to think. As he sunk into the waters, he noticed the water spilling over the edge of the bath and suddenly realized how to use this to calculate the volume of the crown. This was the point of closure, the aha moment, the point of realization. He then ran down the street, naked, shouting, "Eureka" (I have found it).

Second, closure happens when you complete a decision, such as when you say "yes" to the request from another person. Again, it closes off further cognitive effort and resolves associated tensions.

Closure is the brain's way of saying thank you. When you achieve closure, your brain gives you a nice squirt of natural opiates. This is its way of telling you that we are doing the right thing. You feel good, of course.

Closure can be addictive

The closure is so nice we will even seek tension in order to experience the pleasure of closure. Children are naughty to get the closure of attention. Unhealthy habits from over-eating to excessive sunbathing are all driven by the search for closure. Once the habits are fixed, they automatically repeat themselves and can be difficult to stop.

A classic closure-seeking pattern is the drama triangle where, for example, one sibling experiences the closure of persecution when they hurt a sibling, while the other sibling feels the closure of being rescued by a parent. The rescuer can also get closure in the rewards of moral superiority. Such behavioral games are played out endlessly in families, workplaces, and public places.

Addicts find closure in using the needle, even when they are in a reasonable state of mind and they know how bad they are going to feel later.

Re-opening is uncomfortable

When we have closed on something, we feel very uncomfortable if somebody tries to re-open the situation, and we will often strongly resist such attempts. This pattern is typical of beliefs-- when we close on accepting a belief, we do not like having it challenged.

So what?

Closing is a sales specialty and nightmare, which highlights the problem for many -- after all the effort of persuasion, at some time you have to ask for the sale and risk the pain of rejection.

The trick in closing is to find the right time, when the person is sufficiently wound up that all you need to do is tip the scales and they fall easily into the closure of agreeing with you and buying what you are selling, whether it is a vehicle or their salvation.

If you build tension in another person, they will seek closure. This is a core principle in persuasion.

Role playing

My father once told me, "Find out what other people hate to do, do it very well and you'll be a wealthy man." That could not be truer than in the case of role playing. Almost everyone needs it and almost everyone hates it. You will role play, it's just a matter of if you pay for it with cash. What I mean by that is, if you do not role play with a co-worker or manager, you will be role-playing each time you work with a prospect. And if you wait till then, it will cost you a percentage of your commission. Either in reduced gross profit or lost deals. Professionals refine their craft through practice. If you want to be paid like a professional, be a professional. Grab a co-worker or manager and alternate between being the salesperson and prospect. Run through your entire sales process, including the close, and then repeat it under different circumstances. It is best to make mistakes in private, not in public. Don't embarrass the dealership, yourself and/or cost yourself a commission.

Types of buyers

It's important to isolate the objection that is stopping the sale from occurring. Sometimes that's not easy if the prospect is firing offers on multiple levels. Let's run through the basic types of buyers, give you one method of overcoming each type of buyer's objection and then how to isolate demands to one qualifier.

The discount buyer – This person is only concerned about the amount of discount he/she is being given off the price of the vehicle they are purchasing. This usually takes place in the form of a percentage off. For instance, if the selling price is $32,000 then the prospect demands 10% off. Even more illogical is the fact that the selling price has no impact on the prospects' offer (in the prospects' mind). If the vehicle was $23,000 they would still offer 10% off. This usually stems from incorrect information given to them by a third party. That third party could be a neighbor bragging about how great a deal she/he got and exaggerated quite a bit or a site on the internet that says you should always get 10% off. Either way, the prospect has locked this in their brain and it's difficult to overcome.

How to overcome – First, make sure when determining what percentage you are giving off, you include both the discount and the manufacturers rebate and note the combined amount off as a percentage. As an example; let's assume the selling price is $20,000, the discount the dealership is giving off the vehicle is $500, and the manufacturers rebate is $1,500, that is a total of $2,000 off or 10% of the selling price. If the prospect agrees, then close the deal. If the prospect says that they want 10% off in just discount, not including the manufacturers rebate, then you will have to explain that most vehicles, including this one, do not have that type of markup because the manufacturer prices their vehicles to be competitive in the marketplace and that leaves very little markup to negotiate with. And then ask, "So with this in mind did you want to title your new vehicle in one name or two?"

The trade buyer – As the name dictates, this prospect is only interested in the allowance given to them for their trade-in. The figure they have in their mind usually comes from the same places as the discount buyer. This prospect fails to see the defining difference between what they think their vehicle is worth (based on any criteria) and what the dealership feels it is worth. The difference is that the dealership will buy the vehicle and the prospects' informational sources will not. It is similar to having a piece of jewelry your aunt left you and you had it appraised for $10,000. Chances are the appraiser will not buy it for that and you won't be able to sell it for that.

How to overcome – Remember, what you know in

advance you do in advance. If this is an appointment prepare in advance by researching what vehicles like their trade-in are selling for in the market. Whether an appointment or walk-in, you can combat an artificially high demand for trade value with logic. In many cases if you ask your used car manager, or whoever appraises in your dealership, what mechanical or cosmetic issues the vehicle needs to have repaired in order to be placed on the lot for sale and the associated costs, you can deduct these amounts from your prospects offer to arrive at the actual cash value of the vehicle (actual cash value or ACV is the value the dealership places on the trade). In addition, you can also deduct the markup you would add on the vehicle, to the amount you deduct from the prospects offer. Below is an example:

Prospect request for trade - $10,000 (A retail value that you established by showing the prospect your earlier research)

Actual Cash Value - $7,500

Needs brakes - $700

Needs 4 tires - $800

Mark-up added - $1,000

The way this is presented to the prospect is a math problem.

"Mr. and Mrs. Prospect, if you were going to sell the vehicle yourself I'm sure you would get the brakes and tires fixed, right? The tires will run about $800 and the brakes will be about $700. That's a total of $1,500. If we add $1,500 to what my used car manager says it's worth, $7,500, that comes to $9,000. You would need to make some profit on the sale of the vehicle so you would add about $1,000 to the $9,000 to give you a selling price of $10,000 for the vehicle. So you see, my used car manager is giving you what you want for your vehicle but he/she is taking into effect the necessary repairs and markup to make the vehicle saleable. So with this in mind, did you want to title your new vehicle in one name or two?" I am simplifying the process but I hope you get a general idea.

The payment buyer – "I don't care how much you sell me your car for, or how much you give me for my trade, or how long I finance the vehicle, I just want my payment to be $XXX per month and I'll take it." This is what a payment buyer may say. Unfortunately, sometimes these types of buyers are interested in a $40,000 vehicle, have no money down and want to be at $200 per month. I don't care how you cut it, you cannot fit 5-gallons of water in a 10-gallon bucket.

How to overcome – Whenever a prospect gives you a payment offer immediately say, "Up to?" If they did say $200 per month initially, you will get a response similar to "$250 but no more than $260." What just happened? The night before they decided the most they could afford is $250-$260 but they would tell the car salesman $200. When you replied so quickly with "Up to?" it caused them to spill the beans. This spilling the beans just picked up substantial gross profit and/or made the deal possible. All from 2 words! I have literally worked up a budget for the prospects, including taking into account their savings in gas expense from the trade-in to their new vehicle to show them they could afford it.

The invoice buyer – This prospect only wants the dealership to make $XXX over their invoice.

How to overcome – Some dealerships business model is to start negotiations from invoice versus starting from MSRP (or above). If your dealership has its own pricing model don't deviate. Having said that, if a prospect makes an offer of $100 over invoice I would say the following: "Mr. and Mrs. Prospect, the state of (insert your state here) has a sales/use tax of (insert tax % here). Keep in mind that the state does not have to cover our overhead, pay our people, pay the utilities or make a profit from which we take care of our customers. Keeping that in mind don't you think the dealership deserves a percentage of profit higher than what the state gets?" If nothing else this phrasing puts their offer into perspective.

All of these types of buyers' motivation are usually based on misinformation, lack of education, or both. If you have followed the sales process so far this actually becomes pretty easy to overcome. Why? Because the prospect trusts you, and what you have to say. All you have to do is form a logical response to overcome their objection. Keep in mind, though, you have to understand what is logical to them, not you.

Stop the running

One way to stop running back and forth to your manager with a different commitment every time and get all the objections on the table is by using the "other than" question. If the prospect says, "If you can get me $5,000 for my trade, I'll buy now," your reply should be, "Other than the trade amount, is there anything else stopping you from buying now?" This stops you from taking the $5,000 request from your prospect to the sales manager, only to get the $5,000 for the trade and your prospect says, "Oh, I also need my payment at $350 per month."

Finance and insurance

This is the part of the dealership that markets loans and optional add-ons and protection to customers after they have agreed to buy a vehicle at the dealership. At the finance & insurance (F & I) department, customers may be asked if they want to buy optional add-ons like: an extended warranty, auto service contract, credit insurance, or guaranteed asset protection (GAP) insurance.

The F & I department is one of the most important profit centers in any dealership. An F & I manager has responsibilities to the dealership, as well as to the customer and must have a thorough understanding of these duties to achieve success.

The F & I manager's job is to secure each sale and ensure that every vehicle sold is delivered. The manager also protects the gross profit by arranging to finance so outside finance sources do not have an impact on the selling gross. This is the most important responsibility of an F & I manager in regard to the relationship between the sales and F & I departments. It helps to cultivate a team philosophy in a dealership that will ensure both production and profits are maximized.

The F & I manager secures acceptable financing for customers requesting it through one of the dealership's lending sources. Securing financing for customers accomplishes two very important objectives for the dealership. First, it ties the customer closer to the dealership. When a customer finances at the dealership, he or she is more likely to purchase from the organization again as opposed to someone who handles the balance himself or herself. Second, it increases the opportunity for additional dealership income. When the dealership controls the financing, it allows for the opportunity to sell credit insurance products and increases the likelihood that a service contract will be purchased. By handling the balance on the purchase of the vehicle, the F & I department has the opportunity to generate income for the dealership from many different areas. First of all, the lender pays the dealership a finance reserve for handling the contracting and financing with them.

Also, an important profit center to the F & I department is credit insurance that will pay off the loan in the event of the death of the insured and/or make the monthly payments should the insured become sick or injured. Vehicle service contracts, which offer mechanical protection and cover parts, labor, and generally taxes and fluids on covered repairs are also a valuable product for generating F & I income.

Many dealers also offer additional profit opportunities through the sale of products such as GAP coverage, maintenance plans, window engraving, and other after-market items. In addition to generating income, all these products offer benefits to the customer and, in the case of credit insurance and service contracts, protects the customers' future ability to purchase another vehicle.

Once a customer and a deal are turned over to the F & I manager, it is his/her duty to maintain control of all the paperwork until it is ready to be turned into the general office. This means that on a dealership finance deal, control is kept until the loan is approved and all the necessary paperwork has been signed. On cash deals, the F & I manager maintains control until all the money is accounted for, all checks are received, and funds have been verified. On an outside finance deal, the F & I manager maintains control until a draft has been delivered and drafting instructions have been made available. The F & I manager is responsible for all paperwork involved with the sale of the vehicle. This means obtaining customer signatures on all necessary forms and also obtaining payoff and insurance information. In many dealerships, salespeople may perform these two duties. However, it is still up to the F & I manager to explain to the salespeople the importance of the payoff and insurance information and to provide training to the salespeople to ensure the information is gathered accurately and quickly.

Many salespeople don't understand the process of F & I. It is the F & I manager's job to train and educate the salespeople with regard to the inner workings of the department, the benefits of the protective products offered, and the role that salespeople play in the success of the department. One of the best ways to accomplish this is for the F & I manager to be actively involved in sales and training meetings at the dealership on a regular basis.

It is impossible to measure the success of the F & I department if performance is not measured and monitored. Successful F & I managers provide progress reports on a daily basis to the dealer, general manager, and/or general sales manager. In addition, at the end of the month, the F & I manager will complete an end-of-the-month summary to see how well the objectives for the month were met compared to the monthly forecast.

It is important for an F & I manager to be an individual whose work habits, integrity, and ethics are respected by not only the customers, but by co-workers, employers, and all parties associated with the department. This would include lenders, vendors, and manufacturer representatives. A successful F & I manager needs the product knowledge, professionalism, and empathy that customers look for today. In other words, to be a successful F & I manager you must be the kind of person that you would buy the products from and the kind of professional that you would enjoy working with.

The responsibilities of each F & I manager vary from dealership to dealership and sometimes state to state. If there is any confusion as to a particular duty, then it should be put in writing and have the management team agree on whose responsibility it is.

Communication is extremely important to have a successful F & I department because it builds teamwork. It is the F & I managers' responsibility to get the F & I office and sales staff to work together as a team and only by working together as a team can you maximize department income.

11. DELIVERY

"Don't ever promise more than you can deliver, but always deliver more than you promise" - Lou Holtz

The most memorable part of the transaction

Never forget the feeling you had at your birthday party as a child. The cake, ice cream, streamers, balloons, and the anticipation of waiting for your gifts. What a day! That's exactly how your customer feels waiting for the delivery of their vehicle. The excitement is contagious. That is the feeling you want to give to each and every customer that honors you with their business. Never forget!!

Process

After buyers sign the last document, take the new owner on a quick tour of the dealership, paying special attention to the service department where you should schedule their first service appointment. After the tour, go over the owner's manual, instruction books, and service manuals for the new car. (See "how and when to ask for referrals" below)

When the car is prepped and ready for the buyer, the buyer and you inspect it for dents, dings, and scratches. Then go into the vehicle tutorial, which can last from 20 minutes to an hour. During this time, you will walk the owner through all the basics: seat adjustments, power-window operations, and electronics, etc. You should also pair the owner's phone, explain steering-wheel controls, and go over other safety or convenience features.

The more you know your product, and the more vehicles you deliver, the better you become. The experience that comes from so many deliveries translates into more thorough explanations, quicker deliveries and better answers to commonly asked questions.

Customer satisfaction

Customer satisfaction is extremely important. Of course, it is important to the customer, they want to have a great experience when they are spending so much money. Of course, it's important to you, you want your customer to refer their friends, family, and neighbors and you want them to return and purchase again also. It's also extremely important to your dealership and the manufacturer. They want them coming back to that dealership and that brand. When selling new vehicles, you will be measured by the manufacturer and those results shared with the dealership. You will be held accountable, as you should. Do not try to work the system. Use those measurements to identify your areas of weakness and become even more skilled at your craft.

The secret to customer satisfaction is very easy to say and very hard to do. The secret is, exceed your customers' expectations. In order to accomplish that, you have to know what your customers' expectations are and constantly update that knowledge because once you exceed their expectations, you have raised their outlooks for the next vehicle they purchase.

How and when to ask for referrals

The "when" is just as important as the "how". After your customer(s) have finished in the finance office, but before taking them to their new vehicle, use the following word track:

"Mr. and Mrs. Customer, I get a lot of my business

from repeats and referrals such as yourself. I'm going to go in back and get you a small gift (a clean-up kit makes a great gift). While I'm away, if you feel that I have treated you well, please list the name and phone number of someone you think may be interested in purchasing your trade. A lot of times when customers talk to friends, relatives or coworkers about trading their vehicle in their friends, relatives or coworkers may say, 'Let me know before you trade it, I may be interested.' Most customers don't want the hassle of selling it themselves, though. If someone has said that to you, please write their info down so I can contact them. Also, if you would, please write down the name of three people you think may be interested in a new or used vehicle in the near future. Not right now, but in the near future. I'll be right back with your gift." Lay the referral sheet in front of them with a pen and walk away. You will be amazed at how many people apologize for not being able to think of three referrals for you. That's when you say, "That's okay, I'll give you a call in 3-4 days to see if you have any questions about your vehicle and I'll get the other name(s) then."

Another great time to ask for referrals is 2-3 weeks after delivery. It's called prospecting the household and you can use the following word track when you call:

Hi Mrs. Customer, it's Ron from ABC Dealership. I was just calling to see how you and Mr. Customer were doing and see if you had any other questions about your vehicle? No, terrific. While I have you on the phone do you mind if I ask a few quick questions for my records? Great!

a)   How many drivers are there in the house?

b)   How many vehicles?

c)   Out of those drivers, who do you think will be in the market for another vehicle the soonest?

d)   And what year, make and model do they currently drive?

e)   When they do purchase a vehicle do you think

they'll purchase the same type of vehicle?

f) And will they be interested in new, pre-owned or want to look at both?

g) Terrific, if I get something like that in-stock should I call you or them?

h) Thanks so much for your time. As always, if I can help with anything just let me know.

The ten rules of world-class customer satisfaction:

1. *CUSTOMER SERVICE IS EVERYONE'S JOB*
   - Don't ever say, "It's not my job."
   - Be proactive...if you see a problem, take steps to correct or prevent it.
   - Praise, award, and reward...the best generals give lots of medals.

2. *FOLLOW THE "GOLDEN RULE"*
   - Treat your customers the way you would want to be treated.
   - A customer is a person, not a statistic.

3. *DO IT RIGHT THE FIRST TIME*
   - Think continuous improvement.
   - Quality means exceeding expectations, with "zero" defects.

4. *RESPOND WITH SPEED*
   - Do it on time, or sooner.
   - Answer your own phone in three rings and give your name.
   - Return messages within 24 hours.
   - Customer calls/requests are not an interruption. Servicing the customer is the purpose of our work.

5. *UNDERSTAND YOUR CUSTOMERS' EXPECTATIONS*
   - LISTEN to your customers' needs and requirements.
   - Look for opportunities to improve.
   - Measure customer satisfaction.

6. *MAKE YOUR CUSTOMER AN APOSTLE*
   - Build a relationship...become a trusted advisor.
   - Look at things from the customer's point of view.
   - The customer is not an outsider; he is part of our business.

7. *KEEP YOUR PROMISES*
   - Don't promise something you can't deliver.
   - Follow through on your commitments.

8. *HONESTY IS THE ONLY POLICY*
   - Don't be afraid to apologize...own up to your shortcomings.
   - Don't "bad mouth" the competition.
   - Never say no... suggest a mutually beneficial alternative.

9. *STAY COOL*
   - Don't let an upset customer upset you.
   - Listen and empathize with your customer's problem.
   - The customer is not someone with whom to argue or match wits.

10. *WORK FOR THE CUSTOMER*

- Don't expect customers to change to accommodate you.
- Take the initiative to help solve their problem and improve their business.
- The customer is the most important person to our company.
- The customer is not dependent on us; we are dependent on them.
- The customer pays our salaries.

12. FOLLOW-UP

The difference between a five-digit income and a six-digit income (and less work)
Before we consider follow-up, it is important to make sure we have done everything possible to sell the prospect a vehicle while at the dealership. Even if we have done a good job with the prospect and covered all of the steps (introduction, qualification, selection, etc.), averages dictate that prospects will leave without buying. Follow-up is the fine art of turning those walkouts into "be-backs" and ultimately sold customers. Be-backs, previous customers, and referrals close at a much higher rate and are usually more profitable.

You come into work for your 12-9 shift just in time to see another salesperson delivering the customer you spent three hours with two weeks ago. Congratulations, you just learned the value of strong follow-up, or more importantly NOT following up. You need to think of follow-up as putting money in the bank. If you follow-up consistently, when the market takes a downturn, and it will, you will still be delivering vehicles while your peers try to figure out how you're doing it.

Now let's look at the fundamental types of follow-up and some techniques to use:

- Same-day unsold

- 24-hour unsold

- Continuous unsold

- Management review

- Sold

- Ongoing sold

Same-day unsold

Depending on the time of day you saw them; prospects are probably out shopping other dealerships after they left. I am not condoning the following actions but, very early in my career I worked for a dealership that if a prospect left after shopping our dealership without buying, and there was still time for them to go to another dealership, we would give them a parting gift of a half-gallon of ice cream. We would give them time to get home and then the manager would call to see if he could identify the real reason they didn't buy and close the deal over the phone!

Immediately upon leaving, mail the prospect a hand-written thank you card. Many times I have gotten prospects back in that said the only reason they came back was because of that card.

When conducting same-day unsold follow-up, be sure to ask how their vehicle search is progressing. Restate the main points of any offers you made while they were with you. Attempt to surface the real reason they did not purchase and overcome it. Sometimes people will say things over the phone that they would not say in person. Don't put off the follow-up call! A prospect's world does not stop turning just for us. Here are some sample phrases to use:

- Thank you for visiting us today.
- If there was one thing that stopped you from buying today what would that be?
- Are you still considering the vehicle or offer we discussed?
- Are you still in the market or have your plans changed?
- Did you visit any other dealerships?
- What kind of experience did you have?
- Have any of your wants or needs changed since your visit?

- We're here if you need us; I want to earn your business and be your automotive consultant.
- We want you to know that we value your business.
- We want to earn your business.

24-hour unsold

Many salespeople worry about "bugging" the prospect. Prospects do appreciate the calls since it shows that we are sincerely interested in earning their business. Here are some additional phrases to use:

- Would you consider a used (or other) vehicle as an alternative?
- Other prospects have told us that other dealerships did not call them back so I just wanted to...
- I wanted to mention that since you were here, _____ has changed.
- My manager wanted me to tell you _____.
- Factory incentives may change on the vehicle you're looking at (only use this as a last result to surface if it is a price objection. It could backfire and they say they will wait for the new incentives).
- The incentives on the vehicle you looked at are expiring soon.
- We're having a huge sale at the end of the month.
- We have an additional selection of vehicles that just arrived.
- We received another vehicle that might work better for you.
- We received some additional financing information (approval, etc.).
- My manager has a buyer for your trade and would like to reappraise it.

- We received additional factory allocation so we can order your vehicle.

Ongoing unsold ups

Our usual method is to follow-up until they buy or die. While this may seem extreme, it is important to be persistent and keep following the prospect until a resolution is made. Since you will be making repeated calls to the same prospect, a plan is essential.

- Have a fresh reason to call.
- Put the prospect first; it's all about them.
- Ask for a status update (did they buy, are they still in the market, etc.).
- Ask what else can be done to earn their business.

Management review

You should periodically review your unsold prospects with your sales manager. There are several reasons for doing this, which include:

- Make managers aware of details to help one of your prospects in your absence.
- Get a fresh, objective look at a deal or prospect.
- Find a new opportunity to close the prospect.
- Formulate a plan of action to close a deal.
- Make a decision on the disposition of the prospect.

Sold follow-up

Every new or used vehicle customer must receive a follow-up call between 24 to 72 hours after delivery without exception. This is also one of the questions the customer will answer when they receive their new vehicle purchase survey from the manufacturer. Here are the "conversation points" for the follow-up call:

- Thank them for their purchase.
- Ask how they are enjoying their vehicle (not "How is the car running, do you have any

problems, etc.").

- For new vehicle sales, mention the manufacturer's survey.
- If your dealership has one, mention your referral "bird dog" program.
- Remind them to call you with any and all automotive questions (you want to be their automotive consultant).
- Tell them you will be keeping in contact with them on a regular basis and then do it!

Ongoing sold

Once vehicles are sold and delivered, customers should be entered into the dealership database. It is your responsibility to maintain contact with these customers at least every 90 days. Contact can be in the form of follow-up calls, birthday cards, promotional mailers, and newsletters. Ask your sales manager for details and assistance in planning your follow-up program. The most important thing is to stick with it! Most customers will forget the name of the individual who sold them a vehicle before they are ready to buy again unless you stay in contact with them. Additionally, you will increase your odds of getting referral business. Some methods of ongoing sold follow-up are:

- Call or mail cards for birthdays and holidays.
- Send quarterly newsletters.
- E-mail or mail special service offers.
- Send anniversary of purchase cards or letters.

Follow-up, whether it's done during the decision-making process or after a customer buys a vehicle, is a vital part of automotive sales. Follow-up conducted during the decision-making process will increase the odds of be-backs, while follow-up done after the sale should generate referrals and repeat customer sales.

ABOUT THE AUTHOR

Ron Vest, has been delivering fantastic results for the past 30 years. Ron has experience in managing and leading every department in an automotive dealership including comptroller and general manager as well as having served Ford Motor Company as a contract employee assisting with their digital marketing department and Reynolds Consulting as an award-winning senior consultant.

Professional Awards:
Reynolds and Reynolds MVP, Western Region (multiple)
Reynolds and Reynolds Consultant, Highest New Business Sales
Reynolds and Reynolds "Beyond the Call of Duty" award
Reynolds and Reynolds Award for outstanding contributions to the Reynolds team
Reynolds and Reynolds Midwest Regional Rookie Consultant of the year
President's Award (Ford Motor Company)
Honda's "Sales Managers' Guild"
Nissan's "Sales Managers' Guild"
Member of Volvo's National "Dealer of Distinction Committee"
GMAC's Finance and Insurance Sales Award
Cadillac's "Master Manager with Distinction"

APPENDIX

Manufacturer Offer Script

ANSWERING MACHINE MESSAGE

Hi, this is (your name) calling from (dealership).

We have some important information we need to discuss regarding your (customer's vehicle).

Please call me at (your phone #). Again, this is (your name) from (dealership).

Thank you for your time and have a great day.

INTRODUCTION

SMILE – Customers can hear you smile!

Good (morning, afternoon, evening), this is (your name) from (dealership).

May I speak with (customer name)?

If this is a good time for you...Let me tell you why I'm calling. The reason for my call is to make sure everything is going well with your (customer vehicle). Are you still driving it? (If they no longer have the vehicle prospect the household)

I'm so glad you still have it! The reason I'm calling is to follow up on the private offer you received from (manufacturer). Our records indicate (manufacturer) has awarded you an additional $XXX above and beyond all the current public incentives. Many of our customers have taken advantage of this private offer along with all the public offers and fantastic deals we're making here at (dealership name). A good portion of them are driving a brand new vehicle for about the same, or less, than they were paying to drive their current vehicle.

Would something like that interest you?

(If yes) So that we can better assist you, let me ask you a few quick questions...

(If no) Many of our customers that have decided not to get

a new vehicle have passed their award on to a family member in their household. Do you have anyone that would like to take advantage of your $XXX incentive? (If yes, find out whom and when would be a good time to reach that person)

On a scale of 1 – 10, 10 being best, how would you rate your (customer vehicle)?

If they say "10."

Great! What makes it a 10?

If they say "1-9."

That's interesting... Why do you say ___?

What would have made it a 10?

How many miles do you have on your (customer vehicle)?

Since I've got you on the phone, let me verify your address. Do you still live at: (address)?

Is there a better number to reach you?

Email Address: (customer email)

When would you be available...today or tomorrow?

(Follow appointment setting process)

Great! We will see you on (date) at (time).

Please ask for me when you arrive and I'll have everything ready for you.

My manager will be contacting you to confirm your appointment and introduce themselves.   ———

DELIVERY CHECKLIST

PREPARED FOR:

CUSTOMER'S E-MAIL ADDRESS

DELIVERY PERSON

VEHICLE IDENTIFICATION NUMBER (VIN)

Congratulations on your new purchase! Our dealership's Quality Commitment is a promise to do our best to satisfy your total transportation needs. As part of our commitment, we certify that all the pre-delivery items on this form have been checked to help ensure your satisfaction with your vehicle.

Sincerely,

DEALER/GENERAL MANAGER'S SIGNATURE

OWNER GUIDE
- [ ] Owner Guide / Owner Guide supplements
- [ ] Review any applicable Quick Reference Guide / DVD
- [ ] I have personally explained the Owner Guide section on Safe Loading & Driving Practices

DELIVERY DOCUMENT REVIEW
- [ ] Explained delivery process
- [ ] Title document / Financing documents
- [ ] Registration work progress / procedures
- [ ] Extended Service Plan (if applicable)
- [ ] Roadside Assistance Benefits / Roadside Assistance Card
- [ ] Service Guide (Scheduled Maintenance Guide)
- [ ] I have personally explained the any vehicle's limited warranty coverages
- [ ] I have personally explained the Dealership website
- [ ] I have explained that many of these vehicle documents & related information are also available online.

SALE/DELIVERY PERSON'S SIGNATURE   DATE

SERVICE DEPARTMENT
- [ ] Explained service procedures / how to obtain service
- [ ] Set the first routine scheduled maintenance appointment
  Appointment date: _____

VEHICLE PRESENTATION / OPERATING FEATURES
Some features are optional or may not be available with your vehicle.

INTERIOR
- [ ] Keyless entry / key fobs (if applicable)
- [ ] Seat adjustment, memory seat 1 & 2nd row (if applicable)
- [ ] Driver-side or driver & passenger-side air bag
- [ ] Safety belts (adjustable D-rings)
- [ ] Operation of mirrors / Automatic-dimming day / night rearview mirror / heated mirrors (if applicable)
- [ ] Visors & front seat SRS warning for children (if applicable)
- [ ] Ambient Lighting (if applicable)
- [ ] Driver window - one-touch up / down (if applicable)
- [ ] Door locks / windows (power rear window / window loc. switch / flip-out window / power locks / autolock / collapsed rear-door locks) (if applicable)
- [ ] Interior hood, fuel filler, fuel pump shutoff release & trunk release levers (if applicable)
- [ ] Personal Safety System (seat belt pretensioners, fron-limiting retractors, dual-stage front air bags, driver seat position-sensing & crash severity sensing)

SPECIAL FEATURES
- [ ] Audio system / set stations, limit, speed sensitive volume / steering-wheel mounted audio controls (auxiliary audio input jack / antenna location, operation) / audiocassette (if applicable)
- [ ] CD player / CD changer / DVD operation (if applicable)
- [ ] SiriusXM Satellite Radio demonstrated / channel line-up reviewed / favorite channels preset (if applicable)
- [ ] Voice-activated Navigation System with Sirius Travel Link™ / set home address or nearest intersection as Home Destination Reference Navigation Owner Guide Supplement & Quick Start Guide in glove box (if applicable)
- [ ] Temperature, compass, statistics displays, message-center (if applicable)
- [ ] Universal garage door control system (if applicable)
- [ ] Security system operation, including SecuriLock™ & perimeter antitheft systems (if applicable)

EXTERIOR
- [ ] Fuel filler system operation & location of fuel filler funnel
- [ ] Tire pressures review, Tire Pressure Monitoring System (if applicable)

TRUNK / Box and Cargo
- [ ] Spare tire / jack location & operation
- [ ] Liftgate Operation (if applicable)
- [ ] Tire Inflation Kit

REAR SEATING AREA
- [ ] Flexible seating / storage positions

UNDER THE HOOD
- [ ] Fluid filler openings
- [ ] Battery charge indicators

OPERATION
- [ ] Adjustable steering wheel & pedal operation with memory (if applicable)
- [ ] Review payload capacity placard
- [ ] Vehicle starting procedures (starter interlock) (if applicable)
- [ ] Anti-lock Brake System (ABS) / Traction Control System / Trailer Tow prep / Trailer Sway Control (if applicable)
- [ ] Operation of headlights, high beam, flasher, parking, interior, fog lights, auxiliary parking lamps, Adaptive HID headlamps, & Auto High Beam (if applicable)
- [ ] Wiper & washer operation / rear / rain sensing (if applicable)
- [ ] Climate controls / rear defroster operation (if applicable)
- [ ] Review 4WD/AWD operation (if applicable)
- [ ] Advance Trac/Roll Stability Control (RSC)
- [ ] EcoBoost™

ORIENTATION (if applicable)
Driving while distracted can result in loss of vehicle control. Use mobile phones, even with voice commands, & other devices not essential to driving only when it is safe to do so.
- [ ] Familiarize customers with location of controls & commands (location voice commands/steering wheel buttons/audio-handsfree buttons) & information resources (e.g. location of quick reference guide, & owner guide supplement)
- [ ] Demonstrate Bluetooth cell phone pairing procedure (put customer's phone when available & set 911 Assist co)
- [ ] Demonstrate digital music player connection process & location of USB port (use customer's media player when available)

Any Misc. Items (if applicable)

CHECKLIST REVIEW / CUSTOMER SIGN-OFF
- [ ] I have personally inspected my vehicle. It is in acceptable operating condition, and is clean inside and out
- [ ] I acknowledge that all items checked on this delivery form have been reviewed with me by my delivery person to my satisfaction.

CUSTOMER'S SIGNATURE   DATE

Made in the USA
Columbia, SC
13 January 2021